Original title:
Crickets in the Clearing

Copyright © 2025 Creative Arts Management OÜ
All rights reserved.

Author: Lila Davenport
ISBN HARDBACK: 978-1-80567-275-3
ISBN PAPERBACK: 978-1-80567-574-7

The Pulse of the Nightscape

A symphony chirps from the grass,
As shadows waltz, none dare to pass.
Bugs don tuxes, a grand soirée,
With nature's rhythm, they sway and play.

One bug trips on a leaf so grand,
Twirling wildly, couldn't quite land.
The moonlight chuckles, a spark of cheer,
As critters gather, it's laughter we hear.

The starry stage is set just right,
With mischief brewed under the night.
For every slip and every fall,
The night rejoices, embracing all.

So dance away in this twilight fun,
Where laughter echoes and joy's never done.
In grassy halls, where dreams take flight,
We find our glee in the pulse of night.

Harmonies that Hide in Shadows

In the dusky realm where whispers roam,
Tiny dancers find their home.
With each tiny chirp, a note is penned,
A giggle from shadows, around the bend.

They jiggle and jive in the cool night air,
Wearing the stars as their finest wear.
The beat keeps time with thumps and squeaks,
As playful antics fill the weeks.

A brave one leaps, quite out of tune,
Squishing the hornet's dance card too soon.
Yet in this mishap, they carry on,
For laughter echoes till the break of dawn.

Join the ruckus, don't be shy,
Embrace the whimsy as time flies by.
The night is alive with melodies bright,
In harmonies that hide under moonlight.

Nature's Unwritten Cadence

An unseen orchestra begins to play,
Nature's humor leads the sway.
Each little note a chuckling sound,
In grassy fields, mischief is found.

A bug brings snacks, but they all flee,
As raindrops tumble like salty glee.
The wind takes charge, a jester's jest,
Insects giggle, it's truly the best.

With nightfall sketching mischief's tune,
A towheaded beetle brings out the moon.
A ruckus ensues as tunes collide,
With every blunder, we laugh with pride.

So gather 'round, both loud and meek,
For life's sweet chaos is what we seek.
In every chirp lies a story spun,
In nature's beat, we dance and run.

Lullabies in the Night Air

Under a quilt of stars, so bright,
Tiny singers cradle the night.
With stubby legs and dreams of flight,
Their verses tumble in pure delight.

A hiccup here, a squeal down there,
They lose their tune without a care.
Each giggle ripples through the glade,
Where laughter mixed with music's made.

Not far from here, a frog takes a leap,
Missing the beat, it makes us weep.
Yet in this moment of comic bliss,
The night brings laughter in its kiss.

So lay your head 'neath the twinkling sky,
Let nature's lullabies softly sigh.
In every note, find joy anew,
As crickets' wit weaves dreams for you.

Echoing Lullabies

In the dark, a chirp resounds,
A tiny band with no bounds.
They play tunes both late and loud,
To serenade the sleepy crowd.

With violins made of moonlight,
They dance to sounds, a playful sight.
A symphony in evening's grace,
Singing softly in their space.

They keep time with wiggly legs,
While shadows sway like silly pegs.
Each note a tickle in the night,
As giggles flutter, taking flight.

Their laughter weaves through grassy blades,
In this concert, joy pervades.
Hands up high, the critters cheer,
Who knew small sounds could bring such cheer?

The Soundtrack of Silence

In the stillness, a sound appears,
A chorus born from tiny peers.
With playful jests and chirpy sneers,
They craft their tunes to calm our fears.

As night descends, they take their cue,
In rhythmic thumps, a froggy crew.
Sliding and gliding, they sing anew,
Who needs silence when there's this view?

Underneath the starlit skies,
They plot their pranks, with gleeful sighs.
A melody of mischief flies,
As each note twirls and neatly ties.

So raise a glass to those small kings,
With legs that leap and joy that sings.
In quiet night, their jest begins,
A laughter borne from bug-like wings.

Aria Among the Leaves

Beneath the boughs, a jest unfolds,
With every note, a story told.
Their tiny stage of green and gold,
Delivers laughs that never get old.

A concert for the moonlit crew,
With nature's music, laughs ensue.
Tiny toes dance, in morning dew,
To harmonies both fresh and new.

As leaves applaud with rustling cheer,
The night unfolds; the tone is clear.
With each chirp, the world draws near,
And time itself seems to disappear.

So let them play their lively tune,
And bring a smile to every moon.
In wild antics, joy is strewn,
And laughter echoes, like a boon.

Enchantment of the Hidden

In hidden lanes where shadows creep,
Little voices begin to leap.
A gathering fine, their secrets keep,
While audiences of trees just peep.

They tell stories, whimsical and bright,
Tickling toes and taking flight.
With every note, they change the night,
In playful antics, sheer delight.

With mischief sewn in every thread,
The jesters march where others dread.
They twirl around, all laughter spread,
While nature nods, a sleepy head.

So when the evening starts to twine,
Join the fun; it's quite divine.
In quiet patches, they align,
And bring forth melodies from the vine.

Dewfall Aria

Bouncing off blades, oh what a sound,
A leggy fellow leaps round and round.
With a chirp and a click, he's found his stage,
Dancing on leaves, he's free from the cage.

Laughter escapes from the plants all around,
As he shows off his skills on the ground.
He hits every note with a splashing delight,
Spreading joy in the shimmering twilight.

Twilight's Natural Orchestra

There's a fine little band playing near the brook,
With a rhythm so wild, you can't help but look.
They wave their tiny arms, with a ruckus they cheer,
Making music together, oh what a strange career!

They jam under the stars, not a care in the night,
With a sound so peculiar, it's pure delight.
Nature's composers, no need for a score,
They play from the heart, and the audience wants more!

Nature's Nighttime Recital

In the evening air, a tiny tune starts,
With little brown musicians, who all play their parts.
They synchronize hops as the moon shines bright,
Making melodies softly that tickle the night.

A humorous concert beneath the starry veil,
With each joyful chirp, you can't help but smile.
As if the night sky itself is in on the joke,
Chirping along with each playful poke!

Sounds of the Green Expanse

In the open field, where the grass starts to sway,
A lighthearted chorus welcomes the day.
With musical chatter that swirls like a breeze,
They tickle the flowers while spinning with ease.

Every chirp's a giggle, every beat's a cheer,
As nature's own jesters, they all persevere.
With a hop and a skip, they perform and they play,
Turning the night into a grand cabaret!

Blossom and Buzz

In the garden where flowers sway,
Bugs throw parties at the end of the day.
Tiny dancers with legs so long,
Tap their feet to a funny song.

Up and down, they leap and spin,
Drawing laughter, creating a din.
Petals flutter, they laugh with glee,
Nature's jesters, wild and free.

Underneath the moon's soft light,
Chirpy friends come out at night.
With rhythm true, they sing their game,
No one quite knows the tiny names!

While flowers bloom, they bounce around,
A symphony of joy unbound.
In this realm where nature plays,
Every night brings new displays.

The Melodies of Quietude

In the hush of evening's charm,
Creatures gather, making warm.
Buzzing tales with a hint of glee,
A comedy show for you and me.

Beneath the moon, they chirp and clap,
Dancing lightly without a map.
Their tiny voices make us grin,
As if the night's a rollicking spin.

Amongst the leaves, they hold a spree,
Jokes and jests in harmony.
While shadows play, they join the fun,
Hiding from the light, just begun!

The stars twinkle at their show,
In this garden, where laughter flows.
A midnight jam, a joyous plight,
In every corner, pure delight.

Whispers of Night's Serenade

Under the stars, the whispers rise,
Nature's jesters, oh what a prize!
With wiggly legs and buggy wit,
They bring the night alive, bit by bit.

A flick of wings, a little laugh,
They're the stars of a funny path.
In the dark, they tell their tales,
Of silly mishaps and windy trails.

Twirling 'round and jumping high,
They create a show as the moon draws nigh.
A symphony made of giggles and squeaks,
Mirthful echoes fill the peaks.

With each chirp, they spread their cheer,
A comedy club, you're welcome here!
As nature joins in this merry dance,
Every creature takes a chance.

Echoes of Hidden Harmony

In the thicket where shadows play,
Tiny sounds steal the show away.
Unseen performers with quite a flair,
Throwing laughs into the night air.

Their tiny tunes bounce off the trees,
Encouraging giggles with every breeze.
They take their bows, a jolly crowd,
Nature's jesters, laughing loud.

With every chirp, there's mischief spun,
A concert for all, but hardly one.
They dance to a rhythm, quite absurd,
Each little sound, a cheeky word.

In the twilight, they play their part,
Creating a night full of heart.
With echoes of joy under the sky,
The hidden harmony makes us sigh.

The Calm of Countless Voices

In the stillness, a chatter starts,
Tiny creatures play their parts.
They chirp and joke, in endless rhyme,
Mocking the silence, keeping time.

A symphony of squeaks and grins,
Whispers of tails and wiggly spins.
They've no concerns, no cares at all,
Just laughs in the dark, a playful call.

Each note's a tickle, a little jest,
While the moon giggles, it knows the best.
With every chirp, the night ignites,
As shadows dance in the misty lights.

So listen close, hear the silly cheer,
Join the fun, let go of fear.
For in the quiet, their joy prevails,
And life finds rhythm in playful tales.

Reflections of the Evening

As the sun bids its farewell glow,
A chorus starts, putting on a show.
Tiny voices fill the air,
With giggles and whispers everywhere.

Launching jokes on the summer breeze,
Poking fun at rustling leaves.
They jest about the stars so high,
As night descends, they do not shy.

With leaps and bounds, they spin around,
Filling the dark with their joyful sound.
They laugh at shadows, poke fun at fate,
As if to say, "This night is great!"

So pull up a chair, join the delight,
Laugh along with the silly night.
In every chirp, a wink, a grin,
The warmth of joy, where fun begins.

Shadows Play a Tune

In a world dressed in twilight's hue,
Shadows sway with a jig or two.
Voices bubbling with charm so bright,
Spin tales of whimsy, pure delight.

A tap, tap here, a chirp, chirp there,
Who knew the night would be such a affair?
With each little song, a burst of glee,
The echoing laughs bounce back with thee.

Underneath the stars, they unite as one,
Creating memories while having fun.
Each melody shared, a mischievous spark,
As laughter and light frame the dark.

So sway along, let your spirit lift,
Join the jest, a splendid gift.
In this nightly cabaret, don't miss the chance,
To revel in rhythms and shadows that dance.

The Dance of the Night Creatures

When dusk unfolds its magic veil,
Tiny dancers begin to trail.
With little legs and hearts so bold,
They twirl in circles, and stories unfold.

Witty remarks filled with playful wit,
Every chirp's a little skit.
Giggling as they leap and glide,
In the moonlight, they take pride.

Around the blooms, they frolic free,
Sharing secrets, just you and me.
Their fun-filled shows, a splendid sight,
These merry makers of the night.

So let's not bother with serious things,
Join in the laughter that each heartbeat brings.
In this whimsical waltz, all fears fade away,
And together we revel till the break of day.

Twilight's Concert of Nature

As dusk falls, the band takes stage,
A chirp and leap, a funny gauge.
With legs that dance, they call in rhyme,
Creating tunes, oh so sublime.

In every nook, a jest they share,
With squeaks and squeals in the cool night air.
A symphony of tickled sounds,
Nature's giggle all around.

And when one slips, a little bash,
They try again, in frantic flash.
Each note a chuckle, light and spry,
As stars above begin to sigh.

The night is rich with silly cheer,
In the grass, they dance, no fear!
A concert grand, they sing with glee,
As laughter echoes, wild and free.

Voices of the Open Sky

In fields so wide, the chatter starts,
A playful buzz from nature's hearts.
They chirp and mimic with such flair,
As if to say, 'Come join us here!'

The moon peeks down with a knowing grin,
As if it laughs at all their din.
They leap and flap, in jestful fight,
Reminding us, it's pure delight!

They hold a meeting, the night-time crew,
With pings and pops, as they pursue.
Each joke in nature's book unfolds,
The humor here never gets old.

With every note, they seem to wink,
In the quiet night, it makes us think.
What is more funny, us or them?
In this great show, we're all the gem!

The Melodies of a Forgotten Field

In a field that whispers tales of old,
A comedy of chirps, bright and bold.
They gather round, their pipes aflame,
As if they're playing some silly game.

With every sound, a giggle flees,
Like playful whispers on the breeze.
One stumbles hard, it makes a scene,
While others chuckle, so unseen.

From hidden spots, they share their flares,
With pitter-patter, they climb the stairs.
Each note a jest, each tune a jest,
The field is lively, far from rest.

As darkness wraps, the laughter swells,
In nature's realm, there's magic that dwells.
In every song, goofy and bright,
The night unfolds, a pure delight.

Nature's Call to Stillness

The evening hum stirs from the ground,
As little legs leap, a jolly sound.
In this quiet realm, they make their way,
With thumps and bounces, they come to play.

Beneath old trees, a funny strum,
Echoes of laughter, here they come!
With every jump, they twist and spin,
For nature knows just where to begin.

They don the night, a shimmery coat,
In rhythmic ways, they light the boat.
With chirps that dance and blissful calls,
Their joyful spirit fills the halls.

So sit, relax, and join the fun,
For laughter lives where stories run.
In every flutter, every tease,
Nature's whispers, perfect ease.

Whims of the Woodlands

In the woods, a dance ensues,
With nimble moves, they chase their blues.
A chirp, a hop, beneath the moon,
Who knew the woods could sing this tune?

A leaf wears a hat, it's quite the sight,
As beetles groove in the starlit night.
While owls hoot jokes that fall like rain,
The forest chuckles, a merry refrain.

Mice juggle seeds, a tricky game,
While frogs recite tongue-twisters, all the same.
Squirrels laugh as they dart and sway,
Whims of the forest, come out to play!

So listen close, and you'll surely find,
Nature's jesters, oh so kind.
A riot of sounds, a merry spree,
In the woodland's heart, we're wild and free.

The Evening's Crescendo

As dusk descends, the sounds arise,
A symphony of chirps, no surprise.
On grassy stage, the performers sing,
An awkward vibe, yet playful ring.

Grasshoppers leap, and the fireflies glow,
Every little shadow steals the show.
Squirrels clap hands, a raucous cheer,
A band of misfits, year after year.

Twirling stars, they'd improvise,
While the frogs in chorus harmonize.
The moon rolls in, a shiny fan,
A spotlight gleams on this woodland band.

Their antics shift as the curtain falls,
A chuckle echoes through the woodland halls.
An afterglow of laughter's blaze,
As twilight fades in a comedy's daze.

Silent Singsong

In shadows deep, where echoes play,
Tiny critters find their way.
With a hush and a giggle, they softly hum,
A silent singsong, oh so fun!

Pine needles rustle, a laughter's tease,
As woodland spirits twirl with ease.
Each tiny footfall, a skipped beat,
In whispered tones, they can't be beat.

Beneath the stars, they share their jest,
With every chirp, they give their best.
A flicker of joy in the cozy night,
Nature's whispers, a pure delight.

Though silent be their cheerful tunes,
Their joy remains beneath the moons.
In quiet corners, they'll still sing,
A gentle laughter, that's their thing.

Symphony of Dusk

As day turns night, the orchestra tunes,
A lively mix of croaks and croons.
With a wink, the shadows sway,
In this orchestra, laughter holds sway.

Twirling leaves dance 'round the trees,
While playful spirits tease the breeze.
Beetles march in a quirky line,
Each step a rhythm, simply divine.

A woodpecker taps a playful beat,
While owls join in on syncopated feet.
Every twig a note, every leaf a song,
Together, they play all night long.

The symphony swells, the crescendo high,
With bug and beast beneath the sky.
In this twilight jam, we're all in a fray,
A whimsical concert at the end of the day.

Harmony of the Wild

In the night, a grand parade,
Tiny dancers all afraid.
Jumping high, then falling low,
What a sight, a silly show!

With their legs, they start to play,
Sounding off in wild display.
Twirling round without a care,
Making music in the air!

One by one, they take a bow,
Who knew bugs could rock the house?
With laughter echoing clear,
They celebrate another year!

So let's join this merry crew,
Wiggle toes and dance a few.
What a night, oh, what a tune,
Underneath the shining moon!

Lullaby of the Twilight

As the sun begins to wink,
Little bugs start to think.
Planning mischief all around,
To the funny beats they're bound.

Winking lights in concert glow,
A sweet symphony we know.
With a hop and dainty chirp,
It's a grand and goofy burp!

Underneath the moonlit sky,
Pairs of eyes go zooming by.
Little legs in leaps of glee,
Nature's jesters, wild and free!

So, let's laugh and let it out,
Nature's jest is what it's about!
Humming sounds of joy and cheer,
To the rhythm, we draw near!

Shadows in the Grass

In the grass, they take their stance,
Wiggling bodies, ready to dance.
With goofy moves and silly styles,
They bring the night its playful smiles.

Beneath the leaves, a ruckus grows,
Laughing at the sneaky crows.
Bouncing here and buzzing there,
Life is full of funny flare!

Tiny creatures, night's delight,
Bringing joy to the cool night.
They chirp tales of silly strife,
Insects with a zest for life!

So, sway your hands and tap your feet,
Join the fun, make it complete!
Nature's laughter here to stay,
In the shadows, come and play!

Melodies of the Moonlight

Underneath the silver glow,
Bugs begin their nightly show.
With a hop and squeaky tune,
They make mischief neath the moon.

With every chirp, they weave a thread,
Of silly thoughts inside each head.
A symphony of giggles born,
From the dusk till break of morn.

Pairs unite in harmony,
Twisting, twirling joyfully.
Stomping feet and laughter bright,
Together in the soft moonlight.

So, grab a friend and join the spree,
Nature's comedy, wild and free.
With every clash and tricky beat,
Let's dance, oh what a funny treat!

Whispers Beneath the Moon

In the dark, they chirp with glee,
Little jesters, wild and free.
Underneath the silver light,
Making music through the night.

With their legs, they dance and play,
Turning silence into fray.
Who needs bands when they are near?
Nature's laughter, crystal clear.

In the bushes, secrets hide,
Funny sounds they can't abide.
Hopping close, then sneaking wide,
Join the fun, or watch the ride.

When the world is fast asleep,
Tiny voices start to leap.
A symphony without the score,
Nature's jesters—what a roar!

The Hidden Orchestra

In the dark, a vibrant show,
Tiny players, soft and low.
Playing tunes without a plan,
In the night, they start to jam.

Fiddling legs in concert halls,
Each refrain, a giggle calls.
Poking fun at silent trees,
With their whispers in the breeze.

As they saunter on a spree,
Nature's jesters, wild and free.
Catch their notes, a joyous blend,
Where the laughter never ends.

In the shadows, wiggles fly,
Winged comedians on the sly.
Underneath the starry skies,
A concert that ambition ties.

Symphony of the Invisible

In the night where no one sees,
A goofy orchestra will tease.
With a hop and little squawk,
They create a cheerful talk.

Invisible, yet so profound,
Buzzing laughter all around.
Tiny jokes that penetrate,
Hear them chirp and levitate.

Dancing shadows leap and twirl,
Nature's jesters spin and whirl.
Every note a playful jest,
As they play without a rest.

In the moonlit fields they sway,
While the world is fast at play.
A hidden show, a nightly thrill,
An orchestra of daffodil.

The Night's Gentle Pulse

Underneath the starry sheen,
Chirps and chuckles fill the scene.
Tiny pals, they stamp and prance,
In the dark, they steal a glance.

A tickle of the evening air,
Makes their banter light and rare.
With their rhythm, hearts align,
Echoing the jokes divine.

Joking loud where no one peeks,
Creatures shy in velvet streaks.
The pulse of laughter all around,
Nature's jesters wearing crowns.

In the moon's soft gaze they play,
Giving night a funny sway.
A gentle thrum, a quirky beat,
It's a dance you can't defeat!

Tones of Tranquility

In the dark, they sing a tune,
A chirp, a chatter under the moon.
With legs that dance on the grassy floor,
They join a band, they're wanting more.

A chorus made of little strays,
With tiny voices in wild displays.
Each note a giggle, a playful tease,
As if the stars sway with carefree ease.

They argue who's got the better sound,
A high-pitched longing, a low note around.
In this ruckus, the night breathes in,
An orchestra where all can win.

Oh, what a mess, this nighttime show,
As patchwork symphonies come and go.
A raucous play in nature's dell,
Who knew they'd ring their own bell?

The Forgotten Nocturne

With the moon as their spotlight wide,
A jingle here, a jangle beside.
These little jesters of the night,
In concert, brings laughter quite bright.

They leap and hop without a care,
A joking pair dancing in the air.
Each note they strike brings giggles near,
Echoes of joy, not a hint of fear.

Listen close, the tales they weave,
Of midnight snacks and pranks up their sleeve.
A symphony made of whimsy and fun,
Reminding us that life's never done.

On this stage, every bug gets a role,
With belly laughs that fill the whole.
So here's to the night, the laughter they fling,
And these little storytellers that sing!

Humming in the Hush

In the lull of the evening, a buzz ignites,
Tiny marionettes with chittering sights.
Each little chirp like a coded joke,
They'll tickle your ears as the night awoke.

With legs of rubber, they bounce and sway,
A lyricist's dream in a natural way.
Dressed up in shadows, they rule the night,
A whimsical verse that feels just right.

They plan their pranks, though few can hear,
A cosmic game, their voices cheer.
In this charade with wings all aglow,
Who knew such giggles could steal the show?

So if you find yourself wandering wide,
Listen for laughter where the moon does hide.
In a world of whispers where dreams take flight,
You might just join in this quirky night.

A Nocturnal Overture

The night parade with its jolly tunes,
Wobbly rhythms of sweetly crooned spoons.
Each chirp a canvas, colors collide,
As nature's jesters put laughter on pride.

An ensemble of giggles in the moon's embrace,
Little pranksters dance in a frisky race.
Like polka dots splashed on a night so wide,
Their funny antics, oh how they glide!

What are they up to? Who's in the lead?
A jumble of voices, like a comic deed.
In this joyful ruckus, there's magic so grand,
Stimulating cheer at nature's command.

So join the ruckus, entrust your heart,
To the whimsy that drifts in the shadows of art.
From dusk till dawn, let the melody spin,
In the delightful chaos that's waiting within!

Fluttering Notes in the Dark

In the night, they chirp and dive,
With tiny legs, they come alive.
A concert played, no tickets sold,
A symphony as the night grows cold.

They dance around in crazy flight,
Hopping here, then taking flight.
A leap and bound, a silly show,
Who knew they loved the limelight so?

Their laughter echoes through the trees,
With every jump, they tease the breeze.
Each note a giggle, so absurd,
Nature's jesters without a word.

Under stars with mischief rife,
They sing the songs of joyful life.
In the dark, they find their glee,
The quirkiest choir you'll ever see.

Glimmering Sounds of Solitude

In the quiet, they make a scene,
With tiny voices, sharp and keen.
Their calls a riddle in the night,
A puzzling jest, a playful fright.

One hops high, the other sly,
A little prank as they go by.
With every chirp, a comic spin,
The show goes on, let fun begin!

They tickle ears with silly tunes,
Beneath the glow of watchful moons.
Their laughter bounces, crisp and clear,
A silly serenade with no one near.

As shadows dance and laughter rings,
They thrive amidst the whispered flings.
In solitude, their jokes resound,
A quirky chorus all around.

Twilight Serenade

As daylight wanes, they start to play,
With unabashed charms on display.
A jolly band with wild intent,
Their giggles echo, wonderment.

They leap and twirl, what fun to see,
With little hops like jubilee.
Each note they sing a wily jest,
A playful tune, they know best.

The twilight drapes a cloak of glee,
And here they are, so wild and free.
In this show, they steal the night,
A comedy of sounds just right.

With damp grass as their stage tonight,
They frolic on till morning's light.
A twilight serenade unfolds,
With laughter bright and joy untold.

Echoes in the Glade

In the glade where shadows creep,
Little voices stir from sleep.
With a chorus, they take flight,
In echoes bouncing through the night.

A merry band in the leafy shade,
With leaps and bounds, their plans are made.
They craft their songs from blades of grass,
In a silly game that none surpass.

With chirps and chirrups, notes collide,
A playful chaos in the stride.
As humor weaves its way around,
In nature's arms, pure joy is found.

So listen close; don't miss a beat,
They'll keep you laughing, oh so sweet.
In the glade, their tales unfold,
A riot of sounds both brave and bold.

Mysteries of the Quiet

In the dusk, the whispers play,
Bouncing off where shadows sway.
Tiny creatures sing and tease,
Making music in the breeze.

With each chirp, a secret's told,
As night descends, the air turns bold.
What game is played beneath the trees?
Is it truth or just a tease?

Beneath the moon, they spin and glide,
With tiny feet, they laugh and hide.
A lively show, a best-kept plot,
Who knew such fun could be so hot?

As we sit, with snacks in hand,
They conspire—our little band.
Popping popcorn, sharing jokes,
In the dark, we're all just folks.

Nature's Whispers at Dusk

In twilight's glow, the mischief brews,
With whimsical tunes and playful news.
Nature's orchestra starts to play,
Filling the night with a grand ballet.

The grasshoppers leap, the beetles drum,
A night of fun has just begun.
Who needs a stage, when you have stars?
They'll treat us with music from Venus to Mars!

A secret chat in the chirpy gloom,
As shadows waltz to the night's sweet tune.
Invisible walls, they playfully roam,
In this grassy hall, they'll call it home.

With a giggle shared by a nearby toad,
The rhythm builds, their joy bestowed.
In the woodsy cabaret, laughter flows,
In Nature's whispers, hilarity grows.

Sentinels of the Serenade

Guardians of the silent night,
With tiny voices that take flight.
Each note a riddle, each pause a joke,
A symphony spun, a giggling cloak.

In the shadows, their antics bloom,
While stars above wear a sparkling costume.
Making mischief beneath the moon,
With a chorus that hums a cheeky tune.

What tales do they weave in the thick of trees?
Missed by humans, but clear as a breeze.
As bushes rustle and leaves are stirred,
Could it be laughter disguised as a word?

From dusk till dawn, they start to fray,
Leaving us wondering, "What did they say?"
In the cool air, their giggles dance,
Inviting us all to join in their trance.

A Dance of Shadows

In midnight's dance, the shadows prance,
    With tiny steps in a curious stance.
Each flicker brightens the night's parade,
    An unseen show, theatrically made.

They shuffle and leap in the polite dark,
Chasing shadows, they leave their mark.
    What's the punchline? What's the jest?
    In this nature play, we're all a guest.

With insects twirling and whispers loud,
The underbrush forms a laughing crowd.
    From where we sit, the magic thrives,
    In witty chirps, real joy derives.

As morning beckons, the show will end,
Yet in our hearts, the laughter will blend.
With clubbed feet and boundless cheer,
They'll keep us entertained year after year.

Gathered by the Glade

Beneath the moon's soft glow, they sing,
With tiny legs, they dance and cling.
No invitations sent, just pure delight,
A gathering of chirps, in the cool of night.

Their chatter echoes, a rhythm divine,
Tangled in laughter, like grapevines entwined.
Bouncing about, they trip and fall,
A comical crew, they're having a ball.

They boast of tales, of skies so wide,
Each little warrior, with endless pride.
But in their antics, a truth they expose,
Under starlit nights, their fun only grows.

From twig to leaf, they leap with glee,
In this nature's party, they're wild and free.
Join the festivity, don't miss the show,
Where tiny jesters put on the flow.

The Chorus of Nature

A symphony of small, in the night air,
With squeaks and squeals, a lively affair.
Each note a giggle, each pause a tease,
Creating a ruckus with mischievous ease.

They plot their schemes on a mossy log,
Imagining chases, pretending to jog.
But in the moonlight, they stumble and trip,
A chorus of laughter, they can't help but skip.

With winks and nods, they join the fun,
A parade of whispers, till night's nearly done.
They wear their confidence, like a badge of pride,
The rulers of chaos, with nowhere to hide.

As dawn peeks in, their banter subsides,
The wise old owl chuckles, their jovial guides.
For nature's folly is never quite clear,
Just listen closely and you'll burst with cheer.

The Evening's Embrace

As daylight fades, the jesters awake,
With tiny hearts that giggle and quake.
In shadows they gather, a bustling crew,
The evening's embrace, with laughter anew.

Oh, how they chirp, a raucous delight,
Dancing in circles, beneath starry light.
Each little blunder, a comic affair,
In this twilight realm, they just do not care.

While frogs croon softly, they jump and play,
Turning the night into their cabaret.
Who knew such wonders hid in the grass?
Their antics and chuckles, a hoot—and a gas!

So listen, dear friend, as the world hums,
To nature's own laughter, where joy simply drums.
In this waltz of mischief, don't shy away,
Enjoy the jesters, come join their ballet.

Vibrations of the Wild

In the hush of dusk, a buzz starts to rise,
Little comedians with glimmering eyes.
They bounce and they wiggle, with zest and a shout,
Creating vibrations in the wild, no doubt.

With every chirp, they pick up the pace,
A lively concert, a bustling space.
Here comes a waltz, here's a jig and a reel,
Who knew such small things could fake a big wheel?

Old owls doze, but can't hide a grin,
As the tiny troupe's mischief begins.
With silly debates on the best leafy spot,
They laugh till they tire, but still want more, a lot.

When the moon takes a bow, the stage turns dim,
Yet in their hearts, the party won't skim.
For in the wild, where mischievous bows,
The show goes on, as laughter allows.

Secrets of the Meadow's Voice

In the hush of twilight's glow,
Tiny troubadours steal the show.
With legs for drums, they play a tune,
Underneath the laughing moon.

Whispers dance on breezes light,
While shadows prance in sheer delight.
Each chirp's a secret, bold and bright,
A concert for the stars tonight.

They tease the flowers with their song,
As if to say, "You all belong!"
The weeds sway gently in the breeze,
Joining in this joyous tease.

With every note, they sway and spin,
A delightful ruckus to begin.
Nature's jesters take their stand,
Beneath the sky, a merry band.

The Soundtrack of Sundown

As daylight dims, a tune unfolds,
Tiny musicians brave and bold.
They've got the beat that makes us grin,
A symphony from where they've been.

The grass sings back in rhythmic hops,
While daisies sway and do the flops.
The webbed-foot frogs join in the play,
For evening's fun is here to stay.

A chirpy chorus fills the night,
Each note a spark, pure delight.
Their antics serve a funny thrill,
As if the world's a giant hill.

And though the moon may roll its eyes,
We'll laugh along beneath the skies.
For in this meadow, life's a jest,
A vibrant tune, we're surely blessed.

Nightfall's Gentle Melody

With twilight's call, the fun begins,
As little lads on tiny pins
Begin their lively serenade,
In fields where laughter never fades.

With every chirp, there's jest and glee,
A nightly show, wild and free.
They leap and laugh, a merry throng,
Creating magic all night long.

The stars blink brightly in reply,
To this wacky lullaby.
The moon takes notes, sits back to see,
What silly things these critters be!

As darkness wraps the meadow tight,
A tune of giggles takes to flight.
For every song is laced with cheer,
A nightly tale, we hold so dear.

Murmurs Among the Tall Grass

In a woodland cast by evening's hue,
The chatter lifts like morning dew.
A tickle here, a laugh on air,
As dusk unfolds, we gather there.

The playful songbirds take the stage,
With antics that defy their age.
They chirp and chortle, create a scene,
The merriest show the world's ever seen.

The tall grass sways like dancers, too,
In rhythm with the chirpers crew.
Each note a giggle, each pause a tease,
As nature laughs, the heart's at ease.

So when the sun dips low and shy,
Listen close, let your spirit fly.
For in the hum of field and glade,
A joyous world of laughter's made.

The Quiet Pulse of Evening

In twilight's grasp, they chirp and squeak,
Their band rehearses, unique and chic.
Out in the grass, a comedic show,
Dance-offs and duets, a wild glow.

Under the stars, they choose their sets,
Rivalry springs, with no regrets.
With legs a-twitching, they leap and dive,
In this nighttime jive, they come alive.

A passionate croak, a clumsy hop,
Each lofty note makes the tension stop.
Nature's jesters, the world their stage,
In the evening's light, they engage.

As shadows blend, the laughter swells,
Echoing secrets, no one tells.
A raucous night, just let it be,
Where sounds of joy roam wild and free.

Songs of the Unseen Singers

In the dark, they rise with flair,
Tickling the night, without a care.
A chorus rings, both loud and clear,
Echoing giggles for all to hear.

With each sharp note, they paint the air,
Like tiny jesters, beyond compare.
A furtive pause, then back they chirp,
As shadows twist, they dance and burp.

Hidden from view, they steal the scene,
Creating chaos, as if a dream.
With synchronized hops and silly yells,
They weave the tales that the darkness tells.

Flashing their charms, and moving fast,
This symphony of shadows will last.
As laughter trails in the night like mist,
The unseen singers will be missed.

Harmony at the Edge of the Woods

At the fringe of night, where shadows play,
A merry orchestra begins to sway.
Legs that strum in a rhythmic rush,
It's a frolic fest, giving quite a hush.

Beneath the boughs, they bump and grind,
With whispers and chuckles, so unconfined.
An orchestra of giggles, a tune of cheer,
The nighttime rascals hold court right here.

Each chirp a joke in nature's book,
With snickers and jests, they'll have you hooked.
With uncanny timing, they shift and sway,
Sending the moonbeams spinning away.

From the brush or the grass, they find their beat,
A side-splitting tale, complete with sleet.
Harmony blooms where laughter grows,
In verdant corners, their giggle flow.

Serenading the Moonlit Grove

Beneath the moon's eye, they take a bow,
With silly serenades, they raise a row.
Chirps and cackles float into the breeze,
As they launch into song with utmost ease.

Tiny jesters clad in night's attire,
Sounding like kazoos, they never tire.
Each note a riddle, both sharp and sweet,
A playful rhythm that dances on feet.

Under starry winks, they form a crew,
Describing mischief in every hue.
Their tunes bubble up like a fizzy drink,
With legato humor, they make us think.

So raise a toast to this playful throng,
For they fill the darkness with joyous song.
In moonlit moments, let laughter take wing,
Join the wild waltz that the night critters bring.

Echoing Through the Glade

In the night, they bounce around,
Making chirps, a silly sound.
Hidden well, out of sight,
Joking 'til the morning light.

They compete with the breeze's jest,
While leaves giggle, they do their best.
A symphony of whimsy plays,
As shadows dance in moonlit bays.

Mischief wraps the twilight air,
Their banter spreads without a care.
Every pause brings laughter's tease,
A riddle played on gentle leaves.

So if you hear that playful tone,
Know it's laughter you have known.
Celebration of the night,
In the glade, joy takes its flight.

Chants of the Undergrowth

In the thicket, a giggle grows,
A little band with chirpy throes.
They sing of bugs and moonlit feasts,
A choir of quirky, jolly beasts.

Their harmonies, oh what a mix,
A tune that's sure to give you kicks.
Every note a playful poke,
In the woods, no room for yoke.

One tones down, the other swells,
Like silly stories time tells.
With every chirp, a jest unspooled,
Nature laughs, the night is ruled.

So if you wander where they dwell,
Join the fun, you'll know it well.
In the undergrowth, delight is found,
In the laughter that surrounds.

The Secrets of Dusk's Choir

In twilight's grip, a tale begins,
With tiny voices, and playful grins.
Their secrets shared through nightly schemes,
A song of jest, vibrant dreams.

One starts a tune, others join in,
A concert of lively, cheeky din.
They plot and prance, so full of cheer,
With every trill, there's joy to hear.

Whispers float from leaf to leaf,
In this merry world, there's no grief.
Each note a chuckle, every pause a wink,
As laughter echoes, hearts do sink.

So if you stop and lend an ear,
The secrets shared will bring you cheer.
Dusk's choir sings of fun and play,
In nature's arms, worries sway away.

Sounds Beneath the Starry Canopy

Beneath the stars, a gathering hums,
With chirps and chuckles, nobody runs.
Each sound a laugh, a frolicsome cheer,
In the night's embrace, what's there to fear?

A nod here, a wink there too,
As shadows shuffle, the merry crew.
They bounce to tunes that flicker and play,
As starlight dims, joy leads the way.

In this vibrant, silly serenade,
Nature's rhythms never fade.
A symphony bright beneath the sky,
Where tickles and giggles never die.

So join the fun, don't miss the show,
Under the night, let your spirit glow.
For in this space, it's all a game,
In laughter's keep, we all stake claim.

The Secret Symphony

In the hush of the night, a tune does hum,
Tiny maestros, oh, they do come!
They chirp and they chatter, with no care at all,
A grand little concert, just to enthrall.

With legs like violins, they strum their best,
Rivals to Mozart? Well, they might jest!
Each note a giggle, a buzz and a squeak,
Who knew nature's symphony could be so cheek?

A harmony found in a midnight spree,
As they frolic and play, in glee they agree.
The audience giggles, the stars start to twinkle,
While the trees all shiver, and the shadows do sprinkle.

So if you hear music out under the sky,
Don't think it's a fluke, just stop and comply.
Join the wild party, let laughter be free,
For the secret symphony invites you and me!

Nocturnal Ballet

Under a moonlit stage, the dancers prance,
Tiny legs twirl, oh, what a chance!
In slippers of shadow, they leap to the fray,
A whimsical ballet, where bugs come to play.

Their pirouettes spin, a twist and a shout,
Who knew little critters could dance all about?
They glide on the breeze, in rhythmic delight,
A frolicsome frolic in the hush of the night.

With twinkling stars bearing witness, they leap,
As grass becomes carpets where dreams softly seep.
While the owls cheer loudly, translated in hoots,
They glide through the night in their fanciful suits.

So next time you're out, don't miss the affair,
The nocturnal ballet dances in the air.
Join in the laughter, let spirits take wing,
For life's just a stage where the night critters sing!

Conversations in the Breeze

In the cool evening air, a gossiping crew,
Tiny voices are rising, with much joy anew.
From leaf to leaf, their chatter can fly,
"Did you hear what she said?" as they buzz and reply.

One claims a grand tale of love and romance,
While another insists on a showy dance.
With the wind as their guide, they spin and they swirl,
As the trees tilt an ear, for secrets unfurl.

More tales emerge in a jubilant spree,
"A tournament's brewing," they laugh with glee.
"The champion's title is up for the best,
In a contest of chirps — now that's the zest!"

So if you are wandering, stop for a while,
And listen to whispers that make the world smile.
In conversations so sweet, and laughter so bright,
The breeze tells the stories of joy in the night!

Flickering Light and Sound

In the twilight's embrace, the party kicks off,
With flickering lights, they all laugh and scoff.
A symphony rises, a quirky parade,
As the stars twinkle bright, no plans to evade.

Oh, how they rally, a cacophony bold,
Each chirp is a giggle; a secret untold.
They dance through the shadows, so lively and spry,
With music in motion beneath open sky.

The lantern bugs join in, a disco of glow,
Bumping and swirling in a whimsical show.
Each flicker and laugh sends ripples of cheer,
In this bash of the bugs, everybody's near.

So when night takes its hold, don't be shy, my friend,
Join the flickering dance, where laughter won't end.
In this realm of delight, let worries take flight,
For the bright sound and shimmer bring joy to the night!

Banter of the Nightlife

In the dark, they chirp away,
Sounding like they're here to play.
One says, 'I've got jokes to tell,'
Another laughs, 'Oh, do it well!'

A party of sounds, all in sync,
Witty remarks, more than we think.
'You call that a song? What a flop!'
'At least no one's here to make it stop!'

The moon's a spotlight, shining bright,
On tiny critters, full of delight.
With tiny feet and wings that flail,
They dance around like a silly trail!

As laughter echoes through the grove,
They share their tales by the old oak cove.
'You tell your stories, I'll hum a tune,'
Together they spark joy till the moon!

Nature's Whispered Secrets

Hushed giggles rustle through the leaves,
As tiny voices spin their eaves.
One asks, 'What's the latest news?'
Another chirps, 'It's not for you!'

Underneath the stars so wide,
They swap their secrets, full of pride.
'Heard about the four-legged hound?'
'Yeah, he tripped and fell on the ground!'

With a wink, they hop about,
Sharing tales of sprout and drought.
'Last week, I danced on the warm breeze,'
'You? Do you think you can tease?'

Around the glow of fireflies' light,
They crack their jokes, the mood is bright.
As dawn approaches, they take their bows,
Witty chums—their laughter still sows!

The Nightscape's Anthem

Underneath the velvet sky,
A chorus of chuckles flutters high.
Tick-tock said the old oak tree,
'Why don't you come and rhyme with me?'

A rascal quips, 'Time flies so fast,
But listen close, here's a blast!'
'You think you're clever with that line?'
'I shine so bright! You can't outshine!'

In shadows thick, the banter's rich,
Each sound a playful little hitch.
With a skitter and scatter, they roam,
Making the night feel like their home!

As laughter twinkles off the dew,
They spin their tales, fresh as the new.
Ah, the nighttime's silly jesters,
In the backyard, true mind testers!

Flickering Voices in the Shadows

Amidst the darkness, giggles glide,
Tiny rascals full of pride.
'I swear to you, my dance is grand!'
'But can you do it on one hand?'

With flicks and flutters, they play a tune,
Under the watchful eye of the moon.
One says, 'I'm the star of the night!'
The others chime in, 'Oh, what a sight!'

A funny dance, they start to prance,
In the shadows, they find their chance.
'Let's make this the funniest ball!'
'But not so loud, or we'll wake them all!'

Whispers and giggles fill the air,
As nighttime critters dare to share.
With a twinkle, they slip away,
Until tomorrow's funny play!

A Melody of the Morrow

In the field where the shadows play,
Tiny jumpers make their ballet.
With leggy hops and wings that sing,
Nature laughs at the chaos they bring.

A chorus starts with a chirrup loud,
As if they're singing just for the crowd.
Silly dancers in a leafy dome,
Every night feels like a funny rome.

Grass blades sway in a comedic swirl,
As they bounce and jiggle, watch them twirl!
Under stars with a winking eye,
They jest with jigs, oh my, oh my!

Morning comes with a sleepy yawn,
Night's antics fade, but the laughs live on.
In a world where the small things gleam,
Life's silly dance is just a dream.

Hidden Harmonies of the Night

Under the moon, a show begins,
With tiny troops that sport their fins.
They rub their legs in a playful jest,
Making noises like an untamed quest.

A chorus of chuckles, a chirp and a thrill,
The nighttime antics give a good will.
Jumping jivers on a leafy stage,
Each leap brings a giggle, a zestful page.

In this concert where small things sway,
Their tunes chase the worries away.
As the wind joins in, it tickles the air,
We all laugh together, with joy we share.

So as the night wears its silly cap,
Join the dance with a hearty clap.
These hidden harmonies light up the sky,
With every jump, together we fly!

The Whispering Thicket

In the thicket where laughter grows,
Tiny jesters put on their shows.
With buzz and winks and a hop so spry,
They whisper secrets to the night sky.

A tickle here and a nudge there,
Their leggy frolics swirl in the air.
Giggles echo from leaf to leaf,
Nature's jesters defy the grief.

Oh, look! A leap and a twirl anew,
As they hop about, it's a view so true.
Under the stars, all fears they fight,
Each sound a punchline, pure delight!

With every chirp, a tale unfolds,
In the thicket, where the humor holds.
As dawn approaches with its light so fair,
These whispers of fun linger everywhere.

Nature's Nighttime Melodies

In the dark, a symphony plays,
A raucous tune of wild displays.
Little legs strum a catchy beat,
Making the world a dance so sweet.

As the moonbeams try to keep up,
These tiny creatures hop and sup.
Their antics tumble like a clumsy jest,
A nightly show that never rests.

Wings like banners flutter and flare,
As they mix up the nighttime air.
With every chirp, a chuckle's born,
In the tapestry of twilight, they adorn.

So, join the fun beneath the stars,
In nature's concert with no false bars.
Together we'll dance, with glee and cheer,
For laughter's magic is always near!

Whispers of the Night

In shadows deep, they chirp and sway,
Little jesters in the grass at play.
Each note a giggle, a secret shared,
With buzzing buddies, no one is scared.

They leap and dance, a merry crew,
In a comedy show, just for you.
With every hum, a punchline flows,
Nature's humor, the world bestows.

They pull their legs, a gentle tease,
As if to say, "Oh, life's a breeze!"
Even the moon chuckles bright,
At the antics seen this funny night.

So join the mirth as darkness falls,
In a meadow where laughter calls.
With tiny stars and buzzing glee,
Tonight, it's a laugh fest, wait and see!

Songs of the Dusk

As twilight hums its playful tune,
The little ones take the stage real soon.
Tap-dancing near a toad's grand throne,
Mischievous whispers in the twilight zone.

With staccato notes that swirl and twirl,
Like sprightly giggles, they give a whirl.
A comedy act, so wild and free,
In the fading light, a jubilee.

Underneath the stars' bright gleam,
They plot their antics, a cheeky scheme.
The chorus crackles, fills the air,
What a delight, without a care!

So let the dusk bring laughter's cheer,
In melodies that tickle the ear.
Join the fun, don't be aloof,
In this serenade, that's the proof!

Serenade in the Meadow

In the tall grass where giggles swell,
Tiny performers weave their spell.
Hopping with joy, they take a turn,
For laughter and leaps, they always yearn.

With chirps like jokes, they fill the night,
A chorus echoing pure delight.
Every tune a jest, every jump a laugh,
Playful mischief, their chosen craft.

They sing of crumps, and huge wet shoes,
Even the shadows nod with clues.
As daisies giggle in the breeze,
The meadow's alive with joyful tease!

So come and join this lively spree,
Where laughter sings a melody.
In the night's embrace, let spirits soar,
With a serenade that asks for more!

Echoes Beneath the Stars

Beneath the sky, where giggles bloom,
Chatty sprites in a cozy room.
Whispering tales that tickle your ear,
With chubby cheeks and heaps of cheer.

They tap-dance on soft blades of green,
With tales, it seems, they've always seen.
As starlight flickers, they strut about,
In the nighttime jest, there's never doubt.

In rib-tickling beats, they take their stand,
With each little hop, they make you stand.
The canvas of night becomes their stage,
A rollicking script, ripe for the age.

So revel now in this humorous art,
Where laughter flows from every heart.
In the echoes sweet beneath the beams,
Join the fun, and live the dreams!

Choreography of Insects

In moonlight's glow, they dance and prance,
With tiny legs, they take a chance.
In leaps and bounds, they spin and twirl,
A ballet show in evening's whirl.

They chirp a tune that's out of sync,
While neighbor bugs all stop to blink.
A twist of fate, a hop and glide,
With wings that flutter, they won't hide.

Nightfall's Gentle Choir

Beneath the stars, a chorus swells,
A symphony of tiny bells.
Each little sound, a funny note,
As they compose a silly coat.

They serenade the sleepy trees,
With off-beat laughs carried by the breeze.
A raucous song, a joyful jest,
Nature's band, not one of them stressed.

The Call of the Evening

As shadows stretch and day is done,
An invitation, come have fun!
With legs that wiggle, they take flight,
Each buzzing sound, pure delight.

They gather close, they giggle loud,
A bug parade beneath the cloud.
Oh what a sight, oh what a sound,
As silly antics spin around.

Rhythms of the Undergrowth

In tangled grass, the ruckus grows,
With lots of beats, nobody knows.
They tap their feet on leafy floor,
A band of bugs begging for more.

With every chirp, a laugh will swell,
A wacky tune, a funny spell.
Together they hum, a forest rave,
Creating chaos, oh what a wave!

The Chorus Beneath the Stars

In the night, they chirp and jest,
Little comedians, working their best.
With their legs they strum, a silly show,
Performing for the moon, in a cosmic glow.

They don tuxedos, made of grass,
Marathon dancers, with no need for class.
Each tiny tune, a giggle and hum,
Under the vast sky, they frolic and drum.

A tickle of laughter, it fills the breeze,
As they sing songs that are rather a tease.
Neighbors peek out, with puzzled delight,
Wondering what creatures play through the night.

So let them laugh, let them play their game,
In this nighttime theater, they seek their fame.
With ribbits and tap-taps, they hold their own,
Under starlit skies, always in tone.

Shadows of Summer's Lullaby

As dusk approaches, the fun begins,
Tiny jesters dance, with cheeky grins.
The air is filled with chirps and delights,
A melody woven through warm summer nights.

Wings and legs, in a comic ballet,
Creating a ruckus in their playful way.
Swapping their jokes with each joyful sound,
Riffing 'til silence decides to astound.

A nudge from the breeze, a boisterous cheer,
Summer's serenade is all we can hear.
Is it music or laughter, who can tell?
In this lively theater, all is swell.

So relish the mischief that lights up the air,
With a wink and a chirp, it's a true affair.
The shadows dance on in laughter's embrace,
As night wraps them up in its soft, sweet grace.

Cicada Dreams in Twilight's Embrace

In twilight's hush, the giggles arise,
Some awkward fellows with starry-eyed sighs.
Bounding along with their silly old beats,
These critters are true under moonlit seats.

Fluttering wings like a jester's play,
Everyone pauses to hear what they say.
A concert of chirrups, both clumsy and bright,
Tickling our ears through the warm summer night.

They dream of great spoils, a stage and a throne,
But it's giggles and laughs that they'd rather own.
With each little poke, they poke fun at fate,
An ode to the awkward, it's never too late.

So join in the laughter, let your heart swing,
As twilight embraces, they start to bling.
In the land of the loony, where joy takes flight,
Let the laughter ripple through the soft night.

A Symphony of Dusk

When dusk draws near, the jesters emerge,
An orchestra of quirks at evening's sweet surge.
They play with abandon, a raucous delight,
Transforming the stillness into sheer, silly night.

With hops and with skips, they strum on grass,
Each chirp is a giggle, they're having a blast.
Don't mind the rhythm, it's wildly off beat,
It's a calypso of chaos, a viral feat.

Whispers of fortune, in each playful tone,
Each blunder's a treasure, and every slip's home.
They dance through the twilight, a charming charade,
In the symphony of dusk, where silliness swayed.

So raise up a cheer for the night's silly crew,
With wings and with laughter, they know what to do.
In the fading light, let your own spirit shine,
For magic is made when humor aligns.

www.ingramcontent.com/pod-product-compliance
Lightning Source LLC
Chambersburg PA
CBHW071840160426
43209CB00003B/362